John F. Kennedy

Nigel Richardson

Illustrated by
Julian Puckett

Hamish Hamilton
London

HAMISH HAMILTON CHILDREN'S BOOKS

Published by the Penguin Group
27 Wrights Lane, London W8 5TZ, England
Viking Penguin Inc., 40 West 23rd Street, New York, New York 10010, U.S.A.
Penguin Books Australia Ltd, Ringwood, Victoria, Australia
Penguin Books Canada Ltd, 2801 John Street, Markham, Ontario, Canada L3R 1B4
Penguin Books (N.Z.) Ltd, 182–190 Wairau Road, Auckland 10, New Zealand

Penguin Books Ltd, Registered Offices: Harmondsworth, Middlesex, England

First published in Great Britain 1988 by
Hamish Hamilton Children's Books

Text copyright © 1988 by Nigel Richardson
Illustrations copyright © 1988 by Julian Puckett

British Library Cataloguing in Publication Data
Richardson, Nigel
John F. Kennedy. — (Profile).
1. United States. Kennedy, John F. (John
Fitzgerald) — Biographies
I. Title   II. Series
973.922'092'4
ISBN 0-241-12288-0

Typeset by Pioneer
Printed in Great Britain by the
University Press, Cambridge

Contents

John F. Kennedy

1   Ireland, June 1963

On 27 June 1963 at 10.30 a.m. a helicopter took off from the American embassy in Dublin. Its most important passenger had landed in Ireland the day before. Ten thousand people had cheered him at the airport; the Irish President had welcomed him, calling him a man 'upon whose wise and firm leadership hangs the hope of the world'.

It was only a short journey to Dunganstown, County Wexford. Readers of 'The Times' read next day that President John F. Kennedy had come 'to the little farmstead to which his grandfather bade farewell 100 years ago'. The President and two of his sisters took tea with their fifteen Irish cousins, which was served on a round table in the middle of the white-washed farm-yard. He joked with them: 'I want to thank all those who prepared this. We can promise that we will only come once every ten years.'

He then moved on to nearby New Ross, where a park was named after his family. A choir was singing; he joined in and then shook hands with large numbers of cheering schoolchildren. He made a brief speech in which he described how his great grandfather had left Ireland with 'a strong religious faith and a strong desire for liberty' to guide him. These values were still cherished by the Kennedy family. He told them that if his great grandfather 'had not left, I would probably be working over at the Albatross Company (a local fertiliser factory) or for John V. Kelly (a local auctioneer)'.

The crowds loved it — and him. All too soon it was time to leave. Next day he flew out of Ireland. It had been a brief, unforgettable stay, both for the Irish and their visitor. 'This is not the land of my birth, but it is the land for which I hold the greatest affection and I will certainly come back,' he declared. Sadly, he never did; a few months later President Kennedy was dead. He was only forty-six.

2 Childhood

Both sides of the Kennedy family originally came from Ireland. Times were desperately hard there in the nineteenth century; like thousands of others they sailed to America hoping to make a better life. They settled in Boston, Massachusetts. Patrick Kennedy, John F. Kennedy's grandfather, made a fortune as a saloon-keeper and became a major figure in state politics. However, some Boston residents who looked down on the Irish scornfully called him 'Pat the Tavern-keeper'.

Kennedy's other grandfather, John Francis Fitzgerald, was nicknamed 'Honey Fitz' because of his Irish charm. He too became a rich and important local figure as mayor of Boston in 1905 despite his humble, Irish Catholic origins. In October 1914 his daughter Rose married Pat Kennedy's son Joseph. Young Joseph Kennedy was determined to be a millionaire before he was thirty-five, and rose rapidly in the banking world.

John Fitzgerald Kennedy — known to family and friends as 'Jack' — was born on 29 May 1917. There was an elder brother, Joe; two more brothers, Robert and Edward, and five sisters followed over the next fifteen years. In 1926 the family left Boston for New York; Joseph Kennedy was convinced that business prospects

The Kennedy summer home in Cape Cod

were better there and that there would be less snobbery against Irish Catholics.

The Kennedys also owned summer homes at Cape Cod on the Massachusetts coast, and in Florida. Although there were nurses and governesses, the Kennedy parents took a keen interest in everything their children did. Joseph was also very ambitious for them and hoped that his eldest son Joe might one day become President of the United States. One daughter, Rosemary, was mentally handicapped and had later to be placed in a home.

Jack's childhood was carefree and enjoyable. The Kennedy children were brought up to develop their talents fully and never to accept failure. They sailed, swam, boxed and played tennis and football. Joe and Jack competed fiercely against each other; Joe was both clever and athletic and, being two years older, had a natural advantage. There were also frequent bicycle races — the two boys once crashed head-on and Jack needed twenty stitches in a head wound. Every Independence Day, 4 July, the Kennedys played all their summer neighbours at softball.

Jack went to local schools until he was thirteen. He then spent just under a year at a boarding school in Connecticut, but in May 1931 he had a sudden operation for appendicitis. When he recovered, he followed Joe to the Choate School, 100 kilometres from home. Choate had a fine academic and sporting reputation; Jack was very keen to become an American football star, but he was never as good at the game as his brother.

School work was a constant struggle. Jack suffered a lot of illness during his childhood and this may have affected his studies. However, he probably spent too much time on other activities as well. He organised a secret club, 'The Muckers', which played practical jokes on people. Once, when these went too far, the Headmaster summoned Joseph Kennedy to discuss

The Kennedy family

whether Jack should leave.

He stayed, and eventually left in 1935, 64th in a class of 112, and showing little interest yet in politics. He went to the London School of Economics for a term but had to return home, ill once again. He enrolled at Princeton University, but was soon suffering from a blood infection. Rather than starting there again a year behind his friends, he decided to follow his father and elder brother, Joe, to Harvard, the famous university near Boston to study Political Science.

3   Harvard and War

Jack Kennedy entered Harvard in 1936. Joe was having a brilliant student career; Jack was only average academically but wrote for the student newspaper and ran a concert entertainments group. He worked hard at his American football, but then injured his back very badly during a match. This injury was to cause him problems for the rest of his life.

He gave up football and took up swimming instead. Jack was determined to get into the top swimming match against Yale University but he caught another virus and was sent to hospital. Friends smuggled cheeseburgers and chocolate milkshakes in to him, and he kept up his training by creeping out to the pool when no-one was about — but in the end, he did not get into the team.

In 1937, Jack toured Europe — including Mussolini's Italy, and Spain which was torn by internal fighting. Europe seemed to be on the edge of war. The following year Jack's father, who had been a leading political figure in the Democratic Party for many years, was appointed ambassador to Britain by President Roosevelt. Jack persuaded Harvard that going on a fact-finding tour for his father would help his own studies. He visited Hitler's Germany, and was present in the House of Commons when Britain declared war in 1939 after Germany had invaded Poland. The Second World War had begun. Soon afterwards, when the news broke that a British liner had been torpedoed, Joseph Kennedy sent Jack to comfort the American survivors.

Joseph advised the President that America should stay out of the war if at all possible. This advice made him very unpopular in London. Joseph genuinely believed that it was not in America's interests to join the war. No doubt he was also hoping that his sons would not have to risk their lives. He still had great plans for them, and told a fellow-guest at a London dinner party that Joe would one day be President, while Jack would be head of a university.

For his Master's degree at Harvard, Jack wrote an essay called 'Why England Slept'. Later published as a short book, it explained why Britain had failed to resist Hitler until it was almost too late, and as well as discussing his father's views on why America should not get involved in the War, it also looked at the arguments for involvement. Harvard was impressed. His tutor had already reported, 'He has ability and gives promise of development.' Jack graduated in 1940, intending to go into law or business.

He spent 1940-41 studying business and politics in California. War looked increasingly likely for America. Joe joined the navy; Jack tried to, but was rejected on medical grounds. He exercised for five months to strengthen his injured back and joined the Naval Reserve in September 1941. Three months later the

Japanese bombed Pearl Harbour, and America joined the war.

After a year doing intelligence work for the Office of Naval Intelligence in Washington, Jack's friendship with a young Danish journalist began to make his superiors nervous. She was being watched in case she was an enemy agent. Jack was transferred to South Carolina to instruct defence workers on protection from bombs. He wasn't very interested in this new position, but any attempt to find more exciting work was prevented by a major back operation in 1942.

After several months he was able to join an officer training course to prepare for duty in a patrol torpedo boat. To his dismay, he was then kept on as a course instructor instead of being sent for active service. With great difficulty (and some help from his influential father) he was at last sent to the Pacific to command PT-109, with a crew of three officers and ten men. The Japanese bombed and sank their escort ship on the way, but Jack arrived safely in April 1943.

For four months his ship patrolled the Pacific islands, trying to stop secret enemy convoys at night. The weather was fearfully hot, and anti-malaria drugs made many of the crew ill. On the night of 2 August, PT-109 was patrolling as usual. Suddenly a Japanese destroyer emerged from the darkness and collided with them. PT-109 was sliced diagonally in half. The radioman later recalled, 'It hit us like the Queen Mary . . . Kennedy went down, smack on his back . . . It didn't even slow down . . . We never saw the other half (of our boat) again.'

Jack in naval uniform

Jack ordered the survivors to abandon ship, afraid that what remained of PT-109 might explode. But the water was covered with burning fuel so they climbed back on to the hulk and stayed there for hours. Finally they decided to swim to an island five kilometres away. Two of the crew were dead, others badly burned. Despite his injured back, Jack managed to haul one crew member with him all the way.

The first island they reached had no food and water, only coconuts. They swam to another island; Jack and one officer then made for a third. Here they found a small canoe, food and drink and returned to their comrades where they discovered two friendly islanders building a fire for them. Jack decided to send them for help. He scratched a message on a coconut husk: 'Eleven alive Native knows posit Need small boat Kennedy'.

The islanders took it to Lieutenant Arthur Evans who was managing a secret intelligence outpost for the Australian navy. He notified the Americans who sent PT-157 to pick them up. Jack's first, humorous question was, 'Where the hell have you been?' Everyone had assumed they were dead; there had even been a memorial service for them. Now they were heroes. Jack received the Navy and Marine Corps medal for 'outstanding courage, endurance and leadership in keeping with the highest traditions of the United States naval service'.

After some time spent recovering from his injuries, Jack supervised the conversion of PT boats into gunships. In November he took part in the rescue of eighty marines trapped in an island base at Bougainville. But by Christmas his injured back forced him to leave the South Pacific for more surgery. The war was coming to an end, but it was a sad time for the Kennedys. Jack's sister Kathleen lost her husband who was killed in France. On 12 August 1944 came the biggest blow of all. Joe Kennedy went out over the English Channel on a bombing raid on Hitler's V2 rocket bases in Northern France. He did not return.

4 Into Politics

When Joe died, Jack turned away from the law and journalism and decided on a political career with the Democratic Party. While he waited for a suitable opportunity, he worked on a ranch and wrote a small book entitled 'We Remember Joe', a collection of memories of his dead brother. (Tragedy was to strike again four years later when Kathleen died in an air crash in 1948.)

Jack also wrote an important article suggesting that the new United Nations Organisation (founded in 1945) should work out a scheme for world-wide limitation of weapons. In the same year Jack came to England to cover the general election campaign for an American newspaper. He found it fascinating — especially a rowdy meeting at Stoke-On-Trent where 500 miners shouted down the Home Secretary. It was an experience he never forgot.

In 1946 one of Boston's seats in the American House of Representatives became vacant. Jack was a more shy and reserved man than many politicians; he never really enjoyed all the handshaking which they are supposed to do, and he once complained that 'kissing babies gives me asthma'. But he and his family threw themselves tirelessly into the campaign to win the seat.

Jack had several advantages over other candidates. He could remind people about his wartime bravery. His family were well-known in Boston, although not popular with everyone. He had enough money to finance a strong campaign. But he had to convince the voters that he really cared about Boston, a place he hadn't lived in since childhood.

He fought a brilliant campaign in the primary election to decide the Democratic Party candidate for the seat. One evening he called on David Powers, an able young political worker for one of the other candidates. He asked Powers for information and advice; Powers was hesitant to help him at first, but agreed to attend one of Jack's meetings the following week.

Jack was talking to a group of Gold Star mothers, women who had lost sons in the War. At the end of what Powers later remembered as a fairly ordinary speech, Jack paused and then said, 'I think I know how you all feel because my mother is a Gold Star mother too.' The effect was electric; every woman there found that Jack reminded them of the son they had lost. 'In all my years in politics I have never seen such a reaction,' said Powers. He joined the Kennedy campaign on the spot. Jack won the primary, and the later election against the Republican Party's candidate overwhelmingly.

He was in the House of Representatives for six years, serving on committees dealing with education and employment matters. He fought unsuccessfully against a bill limiting a worker's right to strike, which he thought gave employers too much power. He also campaigned to end slum housing. In 1952 Jack decided to stand for the Senate. This would mean defeating the Republican candidate, Henry Cabot Lodge, who was already a Massachusetts senator at that time.

Cabot Lodge was a very experienced politician. Like Jack, he had money, good looks, a fine war record and a long family history in politics; a Cabot Lodge had defeated Jack's grandfather, Honey Fitz, in 1916. However, Jack was not deterred. Before even declaring himself as a candidate, he spoke at meetings all over Massachusetts, and with his father and a group of able advisers backing him, he went on to beat Cabot Lodge by over 70,000 votes. It was a famous victory for the Democrats because in the country as a whole, the Republicans won a huge majority.

As a senator from 1952-60, Jack worked for greater rights for the poor and for blacks, especially in the Southern United States. He supported moves to help senior citizens and farmers. He also wrote a highly-praised book 'Profiles in Courage'. It was a study of eight American senators who each took a brave, unpopular stand on a major issue — so unpopular that it ended each one's political career. The book spanned 200 years of history.

During his election campaign, Jack had met Jacqueline Bouvier, a famous American beauty and the daughter of a New York financier. The friendship began to deepen and once elected, he saw more and more of her. In September 1953 they were married at Newport,

Rhode Island. Twelve hundred guests attended the ceremony.

For much of this period, Jack's health continued to trouble him. In London in 1947 he had developed what was at first said to be malaria, but was then diagnosed as Addison's disease. This means that the body fails to produce adrenalin, a vital substance in blood circulation and muscle movement. It is incurable, but can be controlled by regular medical treatment. Fearful that the news might harm Jack's career, the family kept the details quiet, and were criticised by some people later on. Then in 1954-5 he had to have two more back operations. On all these occasions, doctors feared that he might not survive and he was given the last rites of the Catholic Church.

Jack's speeches in these years were always carefully

Jack and Jackie on their wedding day

researched, but he was cautious on most issues. His critics said he was too much influenced by his father, and afraid of controversial issues. They joked that there was 'too much profile (or self-publicity), not enough courage'. Jack was criticised particularly for being absent when a vote was taken condemning Senator McCarthy, who had led a long persecution campaign against possible Communist sympathisers. But Jack was in hospital at the time.

Despite these criticisms, Jack tried to become Democratic Party candidate for Vice-President in 1956. He narrowly failed; maybe it was just as well because the Party lost the election heavily and it would not have helped his career. Two years later he was re-elected to the Senate by a record margin. He now had ambitions to go right to the top.

5 Running for President

Jack became determined to be the next President three years before the election of 1960. The Republican President Eisenhower would have to step down then after eight years in power. But it would not be easy. Jack would be only forty-three by then; no-one so young had ever been elected President before. He had only a moderate record as a senator. Many Protestant voters would oppose a Catholic candidate, fearing that Church leaders would influence him too much.

During 1957-9 Jack spoke at meetings all over the country in order to get himself more widely known. In October 1959 the year-long campaign began in earnest. His trusted team of young advisers, led by his brother Robert, planned every detail. The advertising campaign would project Jack's dynamic image. Computers would predict voting trends. Opinion polls would be taken in the street to see which way people intended to vote. Television would be used as much as possible.

Firstly Jack had to be chosen as Democratic Party candidate. He decided to stand in primary elections in two states, Wisconsin and West Virginia, to show party leaders his strong support. Friends, family and Kennedy money were all thrown into the campaign, but his victory in Wisconsin was only a small one and he lost heavily in Protestant areas.

West Virginia looked an even tougher test. Wisconsin had been thirty-one per cent Catholic; here, only five per cent of the population belonged to the Roman Catholic Church. Jack tackled the religious question directly in a TV broadcast. Church and State had always been separate in America, and would remain so, he declared. People were reassured and suddenly his opponents looked intolerant and unreasonable. He won a sweeping victory.

Some of his other opponents said that doubtful health made him an unsuitable candidate. But at the Democratic Party Convention in Los Angeles in July 1960, Jack won nearly twice as many votes from Democratic Party supporters as his nearest rival, Lyndon B. Johnson from Texas. He immediately chose Johnson as his running-mate; Johnson was a Southerner, a Protestant and a farmer, so could win votes from people who were not Kennedy supporters.

In his acceptance speech Jack told the Party members that they all stood 'on the edge of a new frontier, of the 1960s, of unknown opportunities and perils of unfulfilled hopes and threats. The new frontier of which I speak is not a set of promises — it is a set of challenges,' he declared. 'New Frontier' was to become a famous phrase in his campaign — and later on.

Then came the contest against Republican Richard Nixon in the Presidential election itself. Nixon was also young, but was an experienced politician. He had been Vice-President for eight years and had run the country

The two rivals — Kennedy and Richard Nixon

when Eisenhower fell ill for a time. All the polls
predicted a very close campaign. Jack stressed the need
for change, and promised to halt America's decline as a
world power which he claimed had been a feature of
Eisenhower's presidency. He spoke convincingly again
on the religious question to a group of Protestant
ministers in Texas. No Catholic bishop would tell the
President how to act, he promised. He won the support
of many black voters when he arranged the release on
bail of Martin Luther King, the famous civil rights
leader jailed for organising demonstrations in Georgia.
But Nixon declared that Jack's promises to end poverty
would cost too much. 'It's not Jack's money, it's *your*

money,' he told the voters.

Jack toured every part of America by plane, train and car; working up to twenty hours a day. There was also a famous series of TV debates with Nixon, watched by 70 million voters. They debated both home and foreign affairs. Neither man won an obvious victory, but on television Jack looked handsome and relaxed, while Nixon appeared tense and ill at ease.

The election result could hardly have been closer. Jack won by only 112,000 votes out of 69 million. Some people actually believe that Nixon should have won; there was a suspicion that some voting papers were lost before the count. Many Protestants did refuse to vote for a Catholic, and it was clear that only a brilliant Catholic candidate could have won.

In the ten weeks between winning the election and taking office, Jack appointed the members of his cabinet. They were mostly able, youngish men like himself. The key jobs went to Republicans; he was determined to choose men of talent, whatever their political views. His brother Robert was made Attorney General, one of America's top law officers. Robert was only thirty-five, and Jack had to shrug off the criticisms of this appointment. Robert was the one man he relied on and trusted completely.

One journalist in January 1961 wrote that the sparkle in the eyes of Jack's new team impressed everyone. Another spoke of how 'the glow of the White House was lighting up the whole city' of Washington. Jack had dazzled America with the possibilities of what might lie ahead. Now he had to show that he could achieve them.

6 Washington, January 1961

Jack Kennedy became the thirty-fifth President of the United States at 12.51 p.m. on 20 January 1961. There had been a heavy snowfall the previous night and it was still bitterly cold as he drove from the White House to the Capitol (the American Congress building) with the outgoing President Eisenhower. There on the steps, in front of a large crowd, Jack was sworn in by the Chief Justice, his hand on the Kennedy family bible. Lyndon Johnson was sworn in as Vice-President.

Jack then made his 'inaugural' speech, his first declaration as President.

'Let the word go forth from this time and place, to friend and foe alike, that the torch has passed to a new generation of Americans . . . proud of our ancient heritage, and unwilling to witness or permit the slow undoing of those human rights to which this nation has always been committed and to which we are committed today at home and around the world.

'Let every nation know, whether it wishes us well or ill, that we shall pay any price, bear any burden, meet any hardship, support any friend, oppose

The thirty-fifth President of the United States

any foe to assure the survival and success of liberty.'

He then turned away from foreign affairs and made a direct appeal to Americans to fight with him against 'the common enemies of man' — tyranny, poverty, disease and war.

'In the long history of the world only a few generations have been granted the role of defending freedom in its hour of maximum danger. I do not shrink from this responsibility — I welcome it. I do not believe that any of us would exchange places with any other people or any other generation. The energy, the faith and the devotion which we bring to this endeavour will light our country and all who serve in it — and the glow from that fire can truly light the world.

'And so, my fellow Americans, ask not what your country will do for you. Ask what you can do for your country. My fellow citizens of the world, ask not what America can do for you, but what together we can do for the freedom of man.'

It was a highly impressive speech. 'The Times' reported that the shivering crowd appreciated the fact that the President had taken off his overcoat before delivering it. The reporter ended: 'The charges made during the election that he was too young and inexperienced for this high office sounded remarkably empty.'

That night Jack and Jackie visited all five of the

celebration balls being held in Washington. 'I think this is a good way to spend an evening, and I hope that we can meet here again tomorrow and do it all over again,' he joked. It was a long night at the end of a memorable day.

7   In Public and In Private

President Eisenhower had been the oldest man ever to occupy the White House until Ronald Reagan twenty years later. Eisenhower and his wife Mamie were a quiet, homely couple and his government style was relaxed. His critics felt that he had spent too little time at his desk and too much time on the golf course.

The Kennedys were the complete opposite. People marvelled at the glittering entertainment that was laid on. The night after Jack's election, singer Frank Sinatra staged a gala concert. Nobel Prize winners were honoured at a White House dinner. Cellist Pablo Casals gave a rare private performance at one of Jackie's parties. The Kennedys, with their enjoyment of books, the theatre and art, made intellectuals feel at home. Some people nicknamed their time at the White House 'Camelot' after the legendary court of King Arthur and his knights centuries ago.

Jackie Kennedy, although only in her thirties, made a tremendous impact as America's First Lady. She was not only beautiful, but also intelligent and cultured. Shortly before Jack took office, she toured the White House with Mamie Eisenhower. Jackie did not like the decorations, faded furnishings or the hotch-potch of furniture which different Presidents had added over the past 200 years.

During the next two years Jackie supervised the complete restoration of the White House, amazing the experts with her knowledge. She wanted it to be 'a museum for our country's tradition, filled with the very best pictures and furniture'. She studied plans of the building's early days and found long-lost items of beauty in the basement. She sent scouts all over the world to buy or borrow pieces from private collectors or museums. The result was magnificent; she then took TV viewers on a tour of the building, describing without a scripted commentary, the improvements she had made.

Jackie persuaded the President to improve the appearance of Washington's buildings. She also encouraged him to dress more smartly than in the days before their marriage. She herself spent huge sums on her clothes — too much for her critics, and occasionally for the President. She was a natural trend-setter. One woman reporter wrote: 'She could be in a barn, leaning on a pitchfork, blowing the hair out of her eyes, and she'd still look like Miss America.' She was a great asset to Jack on foreign tours. People loved her; Jack jokingly described himself in France in 1961 as 'the man who accompanied Jacqueline Kennedy to Paris'. President de Gaulle came to America and declared: 'if there were anything I could take back to France with me, it would be Mrs. Kennedy'.

She loved the outdoor life, especially horseriding and waterskiing. But she was also a very private person and loving mother, who played regularly with her children in the White House garden. Whenever she and Jack went off on foreign trips, she left behind a set of postcards. Each day, one would be given out to the children to remind them that their parents were thinking of them. Some people thought Jackie aloof and distant; Jack had to persuade her to wave to the crowds. She found the continuous one-upmanship of the Kennedy family hard to take. She disliked the endless games of Monopoly and charades and once said that just watching them all wore her out. But she always got on very well with Jack's father.

Life with the President was varied and sometimes unconventional. Secret servicemen guarding him at Cape Cod on election night were amazed when he and the family went out onto the lawn to play touch football as dawn broke. Caroline, three years old in 1960, was nicknamed 'Buttons' by White House staff; they often watched her walk each morning from the Kennedys' private rooms in the East Wing to the President's office holding 'silly Daddy's' hand. She once toddled into a Presidential press conference wearing her mother's shoes. She asked the Speaker of the House of Represent- atives why he hadn't got any hair, and told reporters on another occasion that Daddy was 'sitting upstairs with his socks and shoes off not doing anything'. Baby John, born only two months before Jack became President, was his father's pride and joy; they went down to the local toyshop together on Saturday mornings whenever they could.

Jack continued to suffer with his back. He found it

difficult to sit for long periods of time without a break, and had a special rocking chair to sit in. He swam regularly in the White House pool to help relieve the pain, but he often had to wear a back brace and occasionally to use crutches. Once, special cargo lifting equipment had to be used to get him into a plane.

Like Jackie, he continued to love the outdoor life, sailing, riding, walking and playing golf. He was never musical — Jackie is reported to have said that 'Hail to the Chief', the piece of music often played to greet the President, was the only tune he recognised. However, he did like Broadway musicals. But a President can never relax for long, and is never off duty. Wherever the President goes, guards follow carrying a portable telephone and a slim black case. This contains the secret codes which enable the President to order a nuclear attack in an emergency.

Few Presidents can have ever worked harder. Jackie described her life with Jack as 'like being married to a whirlwind'. His office walls were hung with naval pictures; his desk had on it the coconut shell from his war days, with its scrawled rescue message. He rose at 7.30 a.m. and read five newspapers over breakfast, then often worked from 8.30 in the morning until 8.00 at night. Each day brought a succession of conferences to advise him on key issues; Jack preferred small gatherings to formal cabinet meetings. He did his paperwork at an astonishing rate; he could read 1200 words a minute. 'That guy eats up paper like a termite,' said one harrassed adviser. Jack recognised that television helped his popularity. Viewers were allowed to glimpse both his public and private life in the White House, and he gave televised press conferences and impressive talks to the American people.

Harold Macmillan, the British Prime Minister, got on very well with Jack. He noticed that — unlike Eisenhower — Kennedy was prepared to discuss different solutions to a problem and that he asked plenty of questions. Macmillan thought this was partly due to his inexperience in the early months. But Jack was also a loner. 'Nobody makes decisions for Jack,' said his father. 'He asks for opinions and listens. Then he makes up his own mind.' Jack began the morning of his inauguration entirely alone — at Mass in a Washington church. Some critics say that he encouraged the development of an 'imperial' presidency in which

At a meeting in the White House

The Presidential Office

he had too much power.

The arguments about the Kennedy style will go on. What is beyond doubt is that the White House under the Kennedys was a very special place. One of Jack's biographers wrote that they had a 'power of sharing and enhancing the happiness of others'. Perhaps the best tribute of all came from a senior American politician who later declared simply that 'when Kennedy was alive was the last time I felt young'.

8   The New Frontier

In his 1960 election campaign, Jack had told voters that America stood on the edge of a 'New Frontier'. Nearly seven per cent of Americans were unemployed. There was great poverty, especially in the cities. In Southern States blacks often suffered petty restrictions and were prevented from voting. Many of Jack's supporters hoped the New Frontier would mean dramatic new laws to solve these problems. The Democratic Party had a majority in both houses of Congress, which would surely help.

In fact, Jack achieved only limited reform. This was partly because he was in power for less than three years. He no doubt expected to serve two full four-year terms and hoped to push through some of the more controversial laws in his second term. But it was also because Southern Democrats were very cautious. They had little enthusiasm for expensive government schemes to help the poor; America by tradition was a land where people were expected to look after themselves. There was much suspicion of anything that looked like socialism, and of any attempts to give civil rights to blacks. Jack knew that he had won the election only very narrowly; he would have to proceed gradually if he wanted to win a second election in 1964. Besides some money which might have built the New Frontier, had to be spent on weapons at a time of great international tension.

Congress rejected Jack's plan to create a special cabinet minister for urban and housing affairs; he had hoped to give the post to a black expert. It also turned down plans for a medical help scheme for old people and for increased aid to poorer countries. Increased finance for government schools and colleges was delayed; it was said that giving such money to Church schools threatened the traditional separation of Church and State. There were also disputes over how the government should raise money. The President wanted to cut taxes and borrow more. Lower taxes would give people more money to spend, and would create jobs for the unemployed in making goods for people to buy. But Congress disliked too much borrowing.

However, there were positive achievements. The minimum wage was raised, and there were higher payments for certain groups of the poor and unemployed. Water pollution was controlled; coastal areas of special beauty were to be protected. Some housing and city improvement plans were agreed. Community health centres and arrangements for the care of expectant mothers and young children were improved.

In 1962 the President persuaded Congress to drop its opposition to new food and drug controls. These would protect consumers; a new drug, Thalidomide, had just been proved to have caused some babies in Europe to be born with missing or half-grown limbs. He won power to cut import taxes despite opposition from business and union leaders who feared that more expensive American goods would no longer sell. Jack told them that if no cuts were made, other countries would restrict their own imports from America, thus increasing its unemployment still more. He also took unpopular decisions. A pay rise for postal workers was rejected because the postal service was making only low profits, and steel industry employers were forced to cancel a price rise at a time when Jack was trying to prevent the cost of living from going up too quickly.

Southern blacks fighting for voting rights and equality with whites were particularly hopeful about the new President. Jack was certainly sympathetic to their cause. 'Freedom is indivisible, and when one man is enslaved, all are not free,' he declared. He stressed that wealthy people had a responsibility to help those less fortunate. 'If a free society cannot help the many who are poor, it cannot save the few who are rich.'

But here, too, progress was slow. It took two years to persuade Congress to ban racial discrimination in government housing schemes. Ten thousand troops and national servicemen had to be sent to the state of Mississippi in 1962 to make sure that state officials and rioting white students allowed James Meredith to become the first black to study at the university there.

A year later Martin Luther King decided to organise demonstrations in Birmingham, Alabama, to win the right of entry for blacks into churches, schools, restaurants and public transport. The local police set dogs on to the demonstrators, and King was arrested.

His wife appealed to the President; Jack secured King's release and again sent guardsmen to restore order. Later King and 250,000 people, a quarter of them whites, marched through Washington in a dramatic and peaceful demonstration. 'I have a dream,' King told the marchers, using that same phrase over and over again, 'that one day my four little children will live in a nation where they will not be judged by the colour of their skin but by . . . their character. . . .'

Jack now sensed that decisive action would be widely supported. Americans all over the country had been appalled by the rioting, the bombing of black leaders'

Martin Luther King, the black civil rights leader

houses, and by the violence of Southern state authorities, all shown dramatically on television. He drew up an extensive Civil Rights Bill, guaranteeing equality for blacks in all schools and public places in every state of America.

Even this took a year to pass through Congress. It was only after a bomb in a Southern church killed four little black children at Sunday School, and after Jack's own death that his successor, President Johnson, persuaded Congress to accept the Bill, together with another guaranteeing voting and employment rights. Jack's critics have said that he did too little, too slowly about the civil rights issue, but in the end the Civil Rights Act of 1964 was perhaps his most important memorial.

9 The Wider World

Ever since the end of World War Two in 1945 the two
'superpowers', America and Russia, had been involved
in a Cold War — not actually fighting each other, but
trying to gain an advantage through indirect action in
tension points all over the world. Foreign affairs were
like a chess game with each side waiting for the other to
make a false move.

On the day he became President, Jack Kennedy
received a telegram from the Russian leader, Nikita
Khruschev. 'We hope we shall attain a radical improve-
ment of relations between our two countries,' it said.
Russia also released two American pilots who had been
shot down over her territory and imprisoned as spies.
Jack welcomed the gesture, but soon discovered that
Khruschev could be a very tough opponent.

Jack always knew that he would face plenty of foreign
problems. 'Each day the crises multiply, each day their
solutions grow more difficult,' he told Congress soon
after taking office. On another occasion he declared
that 'Mankind must put an end to war, or war will put
an end to mankind.' But he believed in keeping peace
by making America so strong that her enemies would
never dare to attack her.

The President's warm personality won him friends abroad as well as at home. Visiting Canada in 1961 he emphasised the need for the two countries to work more closely together: 'This hemisphere is a family into which we were born.' Enthusiastic crowds greeted the Kennedys in South America in late 1961, as Jack drew up foreign aid schemes to relieve poverty, in order to try to hinder the spread of Communism there. His excellent relationship with Prime Minister Macmillan was helped by the appointment of a mutual friend, David Ormsby Gore, as British Ambassador in Washington.

A fund of goodwill had been built up which ensured that disagreements — like de Gaulle's resistance to Jack's support for a strong, united Common Market with Britain as a member — did not sour the international climate. America also set up the Peace Corps under Kennedy — young volunteers with medical, teaching and other vital skills working in newly developing countries, especially Africa, for minimal rates of pay.

At this time, the Russians were well ahead in the Space Race. A Russian missile was fired towards Venus in February 1961; two months later astronaut Yuri Gagarin made the world's first manned space flight. 'I believe that this nation should commit itself to achieving the goal, before the decade is out, of landing a man on the moon and returning him safely to earth,' Jack told Congress in 1961 as he persuaded it to increase spending dramatically on space research. The result, the Apollo space programme, was one of his greatest achievements,

Kennedy with Nikita Khruschev

although he did not live to see it. The Americans were the first to land men on the moon — in 1969.

Jack had made an election promise to try to limit nuclear weapons tests. He met Khruschev at Vienna in May 1961, but the Russians were not willing to make any concessions. As soon as Khruschev returned home he announced that a fifty megaton test would be carried out, thus breaking an agreement of 1958 and destroying two years of arms limitation talks in Geneva. Both sides increased their weapons after that, but Jack went on trying to persuade Russia to change its mind and to maintain good relations. He gave an unprecedented personal interview to Khruschev's son-in-law, the editor of a leading Russian newspaper. He also released a leading Russian spy in exchange for another imprisoned American pilot. In 1963 Russia and America signed an agreement banning nuclear tests in the atmosphere or underwater. It was a small step, but at least it was a start. A 'hot-line' telephone was set up between the White House and the Kremlin so that the two leaders could contact each other directly in a crisis.

West Berlin, situated deep in East Germany, had been controlled by America and her allies since 1945. Many East Germans had moved into West Berlin to start a new life in the West; by 1961 the trickle of refugees had become a flood and the East German authorities were seriously concerned. The Russians, who backed the East German government, wanted the West to recognise East Germany as a separate state and they aimed to take over the whole of Berlin. A Soviet blockade of West Berlin in the 1940s had failed due to a huge year-long Western airlift of supplies; now Khruschev threatened to stop Western vehicles travelling to the city across East German territory.

Tension increased all through the summer of 1961. Rival tanks patrolled the border. Americans at home built nuclear shelters, fearing war. In August, the Russians built the Berlin Wall to stop the flow of emigrants. The President rejected advice to smash through it: 'In the thermonuclear age, any misjudgement could rain more devastation in several hours than has been wrought in all the course of human history.'

But he condemned the Russian action in ringing

tones. On a visit to the city in 1963 he gazed over the Wall into desolate East Berlin. 'There are many people in the world who don't really understand what is the great issue between the free world and the Communist world. Let them come to Berlin,' he shouted. 'There are some who say we can work with the Communists. Let them come to Berlin. The Wall is the most obvious and vivid demonstration of the failure of the Communist system. For it is an offence not only against history, but an offence against humanity . . . Therefore I take pride in the words: "Ich bin ein Berliner" (I am a Berliner).' The West Berliners loved it, but the problem remained unsolved.

Jack avoided direct involvement in African and Middle Eastern problems wherever possible, preferring to leave these to the United Nations. But America was becoming more and more caught up in the affairs of the Far East, an area which Eisenhower had warned him could turn into a full-scale war.

Communist guerillas, backed by Russia and China, had threatened pro-Western governments in this area for many years. War in Korea between 1950 and 1953 had ended in an uneasy truce and a divided country. Early in 1961 guerillas swept through Northern Laos and attacked its cities. America had already provided 310 million dollars of aid to resist them. Jack had studied guerilla techniques — the tactic of fighting in small groups in heavily wooded or jungle areas rather than staging a pitched battle in the open. He knew how 500,000 French troops had failed to stop the spread of Communism in the 1950s in South-East Asia. America had no experience of guerilla fighting. He wanted to avoid direct involvement.

But after a cease-fire in Laos, problems shifted to neighbouring Vietnam. Eisenhower had sent 200 advisers to help its government; Jack, fearing a 'domino effect' in which one country after another would fall to the Communists, increased this figure by stages to 16,000. Troops followed; fourteen American soldiers died in Vietnam in 1961, 489 in 1963.

Jack felt that the Vietnamese government had to be supported. But it was corrupt and many of its own citizens hated it. Bhuddist monks poured petrol over themselves and burned to death in protest against it. Other Vietnamese turned to helping the guerillas. In November 1963 the government leader, Ngo Din Diem, was murdered — only days before Jack himself died. Jack had called Vietnam 'the worst problem we've got'. It was no exaggeration. During the next five years America was split down the middle between those who supported and those who opposed its greater involvement in the Vietnamese war. There were terrible, violent demonstrations in American cities. By the time the Americans finally abandoned Vietnam in 1975, 57,000 Americans had died there.

10   Cuba

The President faced his greatest challenge of all in Cuba. A Caribbean island, only 145 kilometres from America, it was a poor, backward country. Cuba was ruled until 1959 by a selfish dictator, General Batista, whom the Americans generally supported because of his resistance to Communism.

Then Fidel Castro and his guerillas won a two-year struggle to seize control. Castro accepted financial help from Russia. He forced rich Cubans to flee abroad, many of them to America. Eisenhower's government had hoped to use these exiles to overthrow Castro, and secretly gave them money and weapons.

In April 1961 1500 guerilla fighters landed in Southern Cuba at the Bay of Pigs. Jack had given the scheme his cautious approval, but the invaders were quickly rounded up by Castro's forces. The invaders' elderly planes were no match for Cuban jets, and the President refused to allow the American airforce to get directly involved. The whole affair was a disaster; the world thought that America had bullied and attacked a tiny, helpless neighbour. Kennedy took the blame publicly, and knew that he had made a serious mistake.

Castro was worried that powerful America would

help to organise another invasion. He therefore accepted defensive weapons and military advisers when the Russians offered them. But when the advisers arrived, they quickly set up zones which Cubans could not enter, and weapons which were for attack, not defence.

On 16 October 1962 an American spy-plane flew over Cuba and took photographs. The Americans had been suspicious for some time about Russian activity in Cuba; now the photographs clearly showed medium-range nuclear missiles. Those in place could already

Fidel Castro

reach Washington; others being installed would be able to reach most Western cities. Bomber aircraft were being uncrated and airstrips were being built. For six days Jack and his closest advisers debated how to respond; other Western leaders were told nothing.

There were three choices: the Americans could do nothing, as they had missiles directed at Russia in Turkey near the Russian border. But this would look very weak. America could bomb Cuba, but if they bombed the missile sites there, Russians would die. There might be nuclear war, and if even one missile survived, it might be sent to hit Washington. Or, America could try to blockade the island.

Jack decided on the third choice — to blockade Cuba. American warships surrounded the island; they would stop any ship with offensive weapons getting through. If a Russian ship ignored the blockade, it would be sunk and war might follow, but the risk was worth taking. Although the blockade would not mean the removal of missiles already in place, it would give Russia time to think.

On 22 October, Jack went on television to tell the Western world about the crisis. Everyone waited fearfully to see what would happen. Russian ships continued to advance. Government officials slept in their offices that night; next morning one of Kennedy's ministers told his staff: 'We have won a considerable victory. You and I are still alive.'

Demonstrators in London and other cities protested against America's action. Then some of the Russian ships suddenly changed course. Were they turning back, or meeting up with Russian submarines? Dean Rusk was one minister who was hopeful. 'We're eyeball to eyeball,' he declared, 'and I think the other fellow just blinked.'

Contradictory messages began to come out of Russia. On 26 October, Khruschev seemed to be offering to back down. But next day he demanded that if Russian missiles left Cuba, American ones must be removed from Turkey. Kennedy ignored this second message, but he promised that weapons and troops being assembled on the Florida beaches would be dispersed if missiles on Cuba were dismantled. An American plane then strayed into Russian airspace and nearly caused a confrontation between Russian and American fighter aircraft. Khruschev accused Kennedy of recklessly risking full-scale war.

Suddenly on 28 October Khruschev announced that missiles already in Cuba would be removed within thirty days — in the interests of world peace. The Russian ships turned back. The blockade was lifted; in November new photographs showed that the Russians were keeping their promise.

Within two years Khruschev had fallen from power in disgrace. For Jack it was a great victory after the Bay of Pigs disaster — as 'The Times' wrote after his death, 'Cuba showed him at his weakest and his best'. He had reacted calmly throughout the crisis, relaxing with his children on the White House lawn, but always remaining decisively in command.

11 Dallas, November 1963

By late 1963 Jack Kennedy could point to a number of positive achievements besides Cuba. His recent European visit had been a triumph, especially in Ireland and Berlin. The economy was improving dramatically. Unemployment had fallen, a Civil Rights law seemed a real possibility at last and the Space programme showed that exciting possibilities lay ahead. The Nuclear Test Ban Treaty seemed like the first, hopeful stage in a continuing negotiation. There was every likelihood that Jack would win the 1964 Presidential election by a huge margin, even though the Republicans were attacking the cost of New Frontier schemes. However two family sadnesses marred his success — the death of his third child, Patrick after only thirty-six hours of life that summer, and the severe stroke suffered by his father, Joseph, two years earlier. Rose Kennedy later described Jack's final meeting with her husband. The President put his arm round his father's shoulder and kissed him on the forehead before boarding the presidential helicopter. He looked back at the hunched figure in the wheelchair and his voice broke as he said, 'He's the one who made all this possible, and look at him now.'

On 22 November 1963 Jack flew with Jackie to Dallas, Texas to plan part of his re-election campaign. They had spent the previous evening in a hotel at Fort Worth where Jack found himself discussing possible threats to his life. There were plenty of people in a Southern city like Dallas who hated his support for civil rights for blacks, and there had been violent demonstrations when a senior Democratic Party politician had visited the city only four weeks earlier. Jack seemed unconcerned; 'If somebody wants to shoot me from a window with a rifle, nobody can stop it, so why worry about it?'

The Kennedys landed at Dallas late in the morning. Their limousine had had its top removed so that the crowds could see the President and his wife clearly on the way in to the city centre. Jack and Jackie sat in the rear seats and the Texan governor, John Connally, and his wife sat in front of them. Secret service agents were in the car behind with Vice-President Johnson and his wife in a third car, followed by all the reporters.

The crowds cheered them along the route. Just before 12.30 p.m. the cars turned slowly into Main Street and headed towards a triple underpass. A large red building, the Texas School Book Depository, stood to the right. Connally remarked to Kennedy: 'You can't say that Dallas isn't friendly to you today.'

Two or three shots suddenly rang out in quick succession. One wounded the President but not fatally — it entered his neck, passed out of his body and went on to severely injure Governor Connally. But the final bullet hit the President in the skull. He collapsed into Jackie's arms; in great confusion the car raced to the

Lyndon B. Johnson being sworn in as President

nearest hospital four minutes away. Catholic priests gave Jack the last rites, but he was already dead.

Two hours later Jack's coffin was loaded onto the presidential jet for the sad journey back to Washington. As the plane flew across America, on board Lyndon Johnson was sworn in by a judge as the new President. Jackie, in a state of shock with blood still spattered all over her clothes, stood next to him.

Later that day, Dallas police arrested a man called Lee Harvey Oswald, on suspicion of murdering a police officer that afternoon. He was then charged with the murder of both the police officer and the President.

Evidence seemed to show for certain that Oswald had been at the top of the Book Depository as the motorcade went past, and his rifle had been found there. At a press conference that night, Oswald denied murdering the President. He was unable to give evidence about whether or why he had committed the murders, as he was himself shot dead two days later by a local nightclub owner, Jack Ruby.

The Warren Commission was set up between November 1963 and September 1964 to carry out an inquiry into President Kennedy's death. It found Oswald guilty and that he acted alone. There has been great argument about how accurate these findings were, and whether Oswald was part of a bigger plot to shoot the President. The strange circumstances of Kennedy's, Oswald's and the police officer's deaths have never been resolved.

*

Jack Kennedy's body lay in state in the White House. A quarter of a million people filed past it to pay their last respects. Troops from all the armed forces guarded it; Jackie visited the scene with her young children. On 25 November the body was taken on a horsedrawn carriage to the funeral at St. Matthew's Cathedral. Eight heads of state, ten prime ministers and representatives of over a hundred nations attended. At the end of the service, Jack's famous inaugural address, delivered only a short distance away less than three years earlier, was read out before he was buried in the National Cemetery at Arlington. An eternal flame marks the spot.

12 Looking Back

John F. Kennedy has now been dead for a quarter of a century. During that time many different views about him have been published. At first it seemed that he would be remembered as a mixture of a saint and a folk-hero, someone who never made a mistake. He certainly won the respect of the world, and achieved considerable success.

More recent books have emphasised his weaknesses. He did have faults. He could be extremely ruthless. Cuba did show errors of judgement before it became the scene of his greatest triumph. There have also been rumours about affairs with other women during his married life.

Since Jack's death, the Kennedy family has continued to suffer from remarkable misfortune. Robert Kennedy was a candidate in the Presidential election of 1968, but he was shot dead during the campaign by an Arab fanatic who thought he was too sympathetic to the Israelis. The only surviving brother, Edward, has suffered a series of family and other setbacks. Jackie Kennedy, who now works for a leading American publisher, married Greek shipping millionaire Aristotle Onassis. He too is now dead.

It is often said that many people can remember exactly where they were and what they were doing when they heard the news of Jack Kennedy's death. Precisely why everyone was so affected is not clear. Perhaps it was his youthfulness and good looks, or his energy and the aims he set himself. His stirring inaugural speech had moved many people, and his handling of the Cuban Missile Crisis had inspired confidence and trust in his abilities as President.

This map of the U.S.A. marks places of importance
in John F. Kennedy's life.

John F. Kennedy seemed to symbolise the optimism and belief in a better world to come which was so common in the early 1960s. Above all, he showed so much promise and carried the hopes of so many people — hopes which were cruelly snuffed out at Dallas. As his brother Robert once said: 'Some men see things as they are, and ask "Why?" I dream of things that never were, and ask "Why not?"'.

The American Government System

America is governed by a President. Elections take place every four years. No President may serve for more than two full terms, eight years. Each party chooses its candidate for the Presidency at a Party Convention (meeting). The candidate then chooses his own 'running mate' or candidate for Vice-President. They campaign in the election as a team.

Some states, but not all, hold primary elections before the Party Conventions. These give members of one of the political parties the chance to vote on who they would like their candidate to be for the Presidency and for other posts in the next full-scale elections.

If the President dies or resigns, the Vice-President automatically takes over until the next Presidential election is due.

Most of the President's decisions have to be approved by Congress, the American parliament. In the upper house, senators are elected for six years; in the lower one, representatives are elected for two years. The individual states, e.g. Texas, have much greater powers than a county council in Britain, although Congress passes the laws which affect the whole country. Each state has an elected governor and assembly, or 'parliament' of its own.

There are two main political parties in America, Democrat and Republican. Because Presidential, Congressional and State elections are separate, it is quite possible to have a President from one party and a majority in Congress, or a State governor, from the other. This can cause disagreements.

America, unlike Britain, has a written constitution — a list of government aims and principles. A Supreme Court of nine judges has to see that decisions made by the President and laws passed by Congress do not contradict the Constitution. Congress can make alterations to the Constitution, but they are rare — and it needs a two-thirds majority in both houses and the agreement of three-quarters of the States to do so.

Important events in the life of
John F. Kennedy

1917 Born on 29 May in Boston, Massachusetts

1935 Graduated from the Choate School

1940 Graduated from Harvard University

1943 Commander of Patrol Torpedo boat PT-109, sunk in the Pacific

1946 Elected to the House of Representatives

1952 Elected to the Senate

1953 Marriage to Jacqueline Bouvier

1960 Elected President

1961-3 President of the United States

1962 Cuban Missile Crisis

1963 Assassinated at Dallas, Texas on 22 November